Honoring the Journey:
A Guided Path Through Pet Loss

Written by

KaLee R. Pasek, DVM

Illustrations by:

Kim Cyprian

Table of Contents

Because each person's path to healing and transformation differs, the chapters in this book are a guideline to the process. As Sameet Kumar describes in his book *Grieving Mindfully*, the path of healing is like a spiral staircase circling back to revisit aspects of grief. In this spirit, you may find it helpful to revisit certain sections of this book as the need arises.

Foreword
Words from the Illustrator

I was approached by Dr. Pasek with this project while working as a senior technician assistant at a veterinary clinic. It was there that I experienced firsthand the effects of losing a loved animal and the impact loss can have on individuals and families. This fueled my inspiration for the illustrations, which came from a shared personal understanding of loss, allowing me to convey through expressive color, composition, and body language the path unfolding from beginning to end in text and illustration. Working with watercolor and black charcoal supplied a softness in which the emotions could be expressed without overwhelming the ideas. The pointillism likewise allowed the expression of the unpredictable, devastating, and at times defeating surges of emotion.

I wanted to illustrate a universal "Entity" to which all persons could relate and to represent an individual's inner feelings on the path of loss. The Entity shows the strength and beauty of friendship and the relationship of two beings—the relationship between the pet owner and the beloved "Friend." The lost Friend is shown through a recurring color, a soothing and strong blue as either hints, or swipes, which can provide an environmental and spiritual presence or a concrete figure. This solid figure, a sphere with an infinity symbol lying within, represents the everlasting love and friendship between an individual and pet. Similarly, the Friend's color is evident throughout much of the chapters in that it is a part of the Entity's heart and mind on the healing journey, emphasizing the sense of obsession and connection one feels with what is lost.

The style in each chapter also changes in one or more aspects to show the different stages of loss within oneself. Chapter One's fluctuation within the Entity's core color displays the instability of self during loss; likewise, there is an erratic use of pointillism and indigo, expressive of chaos and depression, illustrating the overpowering and uncontrollable aspects of pure emotion. Chapter Two provides more concrete content, which shows the reality of experiencing loss and incorporates the Friend's color and pointillism used as accents of memories in each illustration, thereby focusing more on the Friend. In Chapter Three there is an ever-present unbalanced heart lying within the Entity's core to symbolize the unbalanced soul of the broken human heart, which later becomes whole. The Friend's color is incorporated into each of those incomplete hearts to describe the pain of love while the Entity begins to take on a continuous color, slowly gaining control and understanding the emotions. Chapter Four introduces the use of solid lines, which shows the fullness of the connection shared by the human and Friend regardless of physical distance. The Friend's color is present in each illustration as a comfort in knowing what was. Finally, Chapter 5 is freed from pointillism and indigo, which both symbolize the beginning stages of loss: depression and emotional inconsistency. Although the pet owner is now able to move on, the love shared is not forgotten, which is shown through hints of the soft, blue Friend color. The Entity is now a steady, strong color as the healing process comes to a close while each illustration holds comforting colors of warmth to remind us of the joys in memories past, present, and future.

This book closes with a frame requesting a picture of the reader's lost loved friend to signify the final process of honoring the journey: to remember with fondness and love the memories shared.

Kim Cyprian, Illustrator

Preface

You have just lost someone in your life who is very important to you. Each experience of loss is unique, and processing the death of a beloved pet can be a very difficult, heartbreaking experience. Feelings of loss occur when we lose someone or something that we love. Losing a pet is no different. Some may not understand this type of loss, and you may not yet even fully understand why this event has elicited so many feelings.

This book is not about the recovery from grief, but about your path to healing. The layout of this book is designed to assist you through the journey - page by page and day by day. Move through this guided path as slowly as you wish. Be with each page as it resonates with you; think and contemplate the words and emotions. Some paths may be straight, others rocky, and others seem only to go up hill. Honor your individual journey. For it is by honoring that you will heal.

As you walk this path I encourage you to reach out to your support system of friends, family members, and professionals who truly understand, acknowledge, and respect this grieving process. Additional resources are provided at the end of this book for your convenience.

My wish for you is that somehow these words and illustrations will assist you on your individual journey to peace and transformation.

Chapter 1

The Reality of Loss

Grief is like the ocean; it comes in waves ebbing and flowing.
Sometimes the water is calm, and sometimes it is overwhelming.
All we can do is learn to swim.

Vicki Harrison

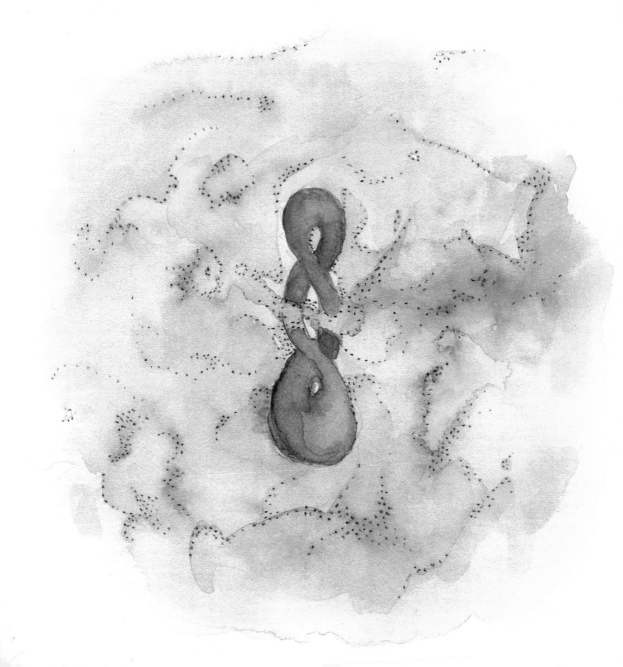

I feel a rush of emotion. Why is it so intense?

I honor my journey: I will allow myself to feel.

The pain of loss often feels initially overwhelming. Do not shut off these feelings. Understand that it is normal to feel a myriad of feelings. Common feelings experienced during grief are anger, guilt, sadness, hopelessness, abandonment, depression, loneliness, victimization, irritability, and intolerance. To express your feelings and talk about your feelings is part of the path to healing.

I shouldn't be so upset. People go through far worse things. Why am I feeling this way?

I honor my journey: I will be with these feelings and will not judge.

Sometimes we are surprised by the emotions that surface. Honor them and be with them. Loss is an emotional process, and the mind tries to make sense of deep feelings by judging. The emotions of loss cannot be reconciled by the mind; rather, they must be processed by your body and through your emotions.

I feel this hole inside of me. How will I get through this?

I honor my journey by taking in a deep breath, allowing my abdomen to extend with each inhale, and breathing in for a count of 6. I will then exhale slowly for a count of 10. I will repeat this for 5 minutes when I feel overwhelmed with grief.

Studies show that during times of loss, anxiety, or stress, your breath becomes shallow from the release of stress hormones in your body. Deep breathing resets your physiology to its natural, calmer state.

It all seems so surreal. I can't believe my precious one is gone!

I honor my journey: I acknowledge that life will be different from the way it was.

This altered state of consciousness is common during times of loss and can occur at the time of a diagnosis or trauma. It is a state of heightened awareness. This is your mind's way of coping. The path that you are on belongs to your emotional body. Be here—now.

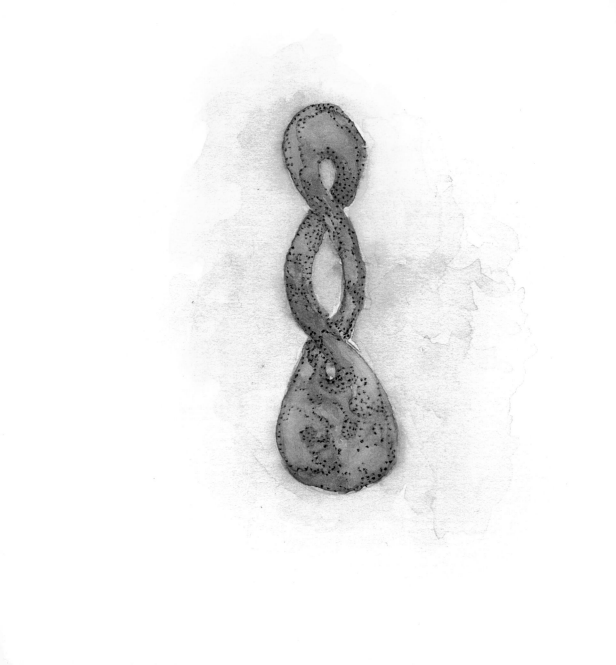

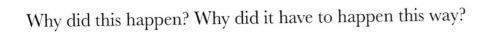

Why did this happen? Why did it have to happen this way?

I honor my journey: I accept that I do not need to know why. I will replace these questions with gratefulness for what I know is good.

As hard as this is, you don't need to understand why. Understanding eases the mind, but grief and all of these feelings occur in the heart. The need for the mind to understand does not ease the ache in your heart. Only by experiencing the feelings will you be able to move along your path to healing.

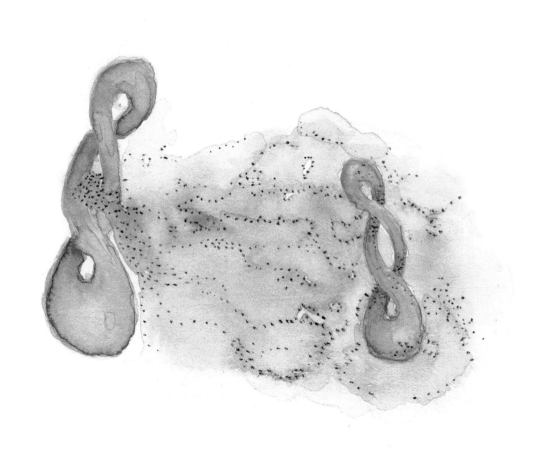

I feel so empty and so alone.

I honor my journey by reaching out to others in my time of grief.

Comfort comes in knowing that you are not alone in your grief.
Many pet owners go through intense feelings of loss when their pet
dies. Reaching out and talking with those who understand your loss
will help you.

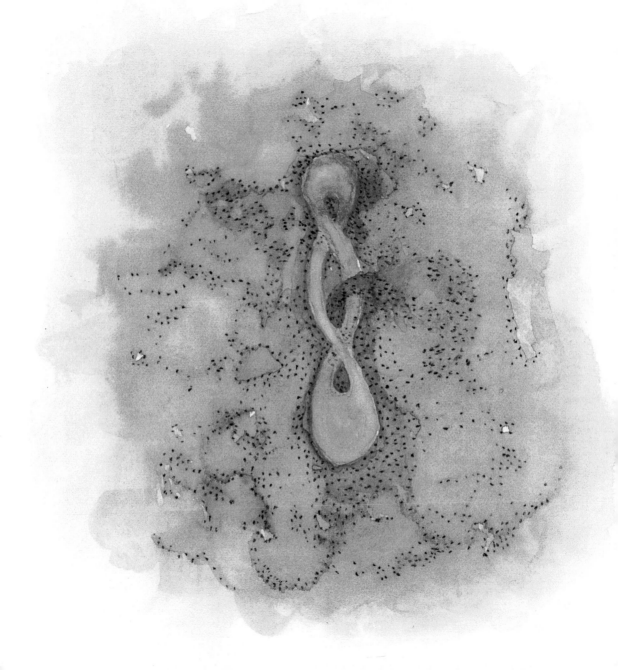

I sometimes feel anger and want to blame someone for circumstances surrounding my pet's death.

I honor my journey: I will express my emotions of anger without being destructive to others or to myself.

Feelings of anger and the need to blame are common during this time. Anger is often an easier emotion to express and be with than the pain and loss that you are feeling. Appropriate expressions of anger can be a necessary part of your healing process. Blaming has ties with the past and shifts the emotion away from your taking responsibility for what you are feeling. Your ability to transform this emotional fuel to healing energy only comes by first claiming this emotion as your own while not blaming others.

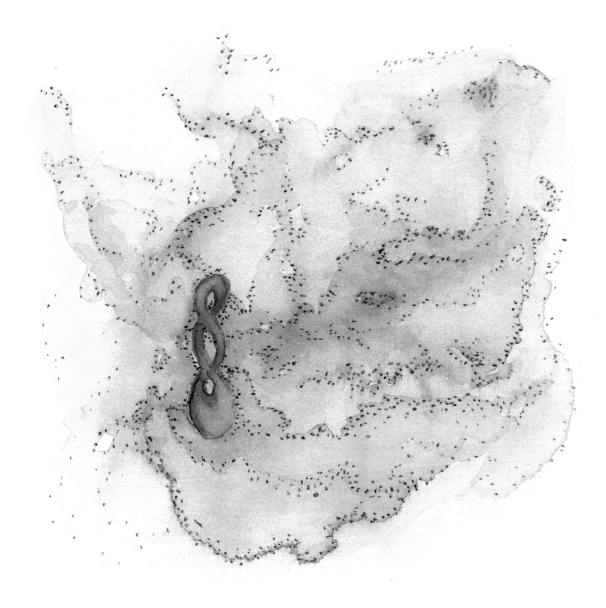

Confusion and disorientation make me feel out of control.

I honor my journey: I will take a deep breath and acknowledge the loss that I am feeling and go back to page 4 and breathe.

It is common to feel confused and disoriented during times of stress and loss. Be patient with yourself and know that these altered states of confusion, disorientation, and sometimes lack of productivity are only temporary. More clarity will come as you move along the path.

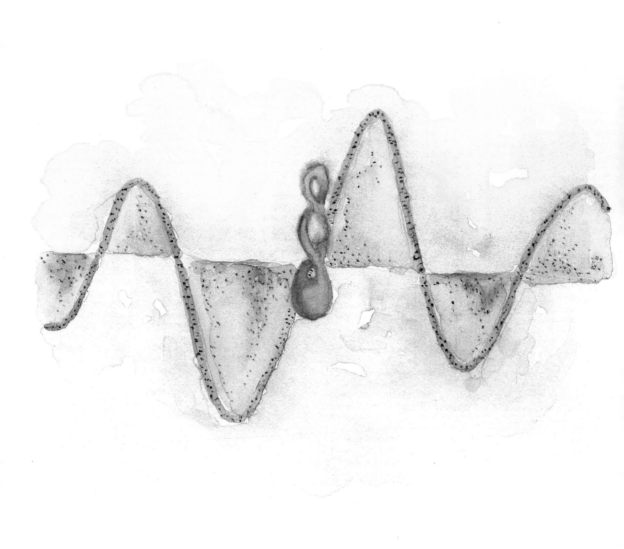

Why can't things be the same? Why did this have to happen?

I honor my journey: I acknowledge this loss as real, and that change is difficult.

Our human nature wants everything to stay the same, but change is a part of life. Life and death are part of this cycle, but the love you have for your pet lives on forever.

I feel this deep sense of pain. What do I do with the pain?

I honor my journey: I am an observer of my circumstance and will call a friend if the pain is too intense because a word of compassion or a hug goes a long way.

Feel the pain, but know that you are not the pain. You are experiencing the feelings of losing someone you love deeply. Although these feeling can be intense, do not define yourself by this experience. Step back and be the observer of your sadness and grief. Go back to page four and breathe. Find the place in your body that feels the most pain and allow your inhale to wash over the pain and your exhale to release some of the pain that you are feeling. Repeat this until the tightness releases.

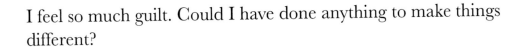

I feel so much guilt. Could I have done anything to make things different?

I honor my journey: I will replace the guilt with self-love and acceptance.

It may be possible that some things could have been different, or it may be possible that nothing could have changed the outcome. Either way, guilt and regret can hold you in the past, obscuring your vision of the path ahead. Accept the present moment and shift your focus forward so that you may walk past the guilt sprinkled on the path.

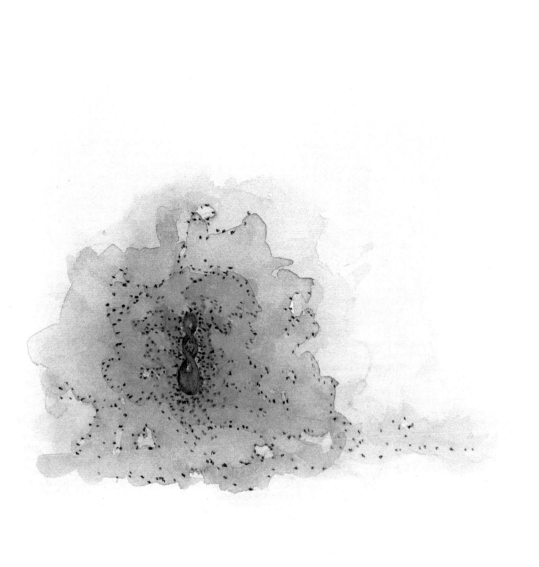

I have feelings of fear and isolation. Does anybody understand what I am going through?

I honor my journey: I reach out to others during times of feeling fear and isolation.

Choose a family member or a friend who can appreciate your loss. Joining a pet loss support group is a great place to find others who feel the way you do. Support phone numbers are listed at the end of this book.

I sometimes feel my pet's presence in the room. Am I going crazy?

I honor my journey: I will find comfort in feeling that my pet is still with me.

Many people feel the presence of a parted loved one long after they are gone. Many different psychological and/or spiritual explanations exist for why this occurs. However, none need to be analyzed, you should take comfort in knowing that this is a common phenomenon and is part of the state of heightened awareness that comes with grief.

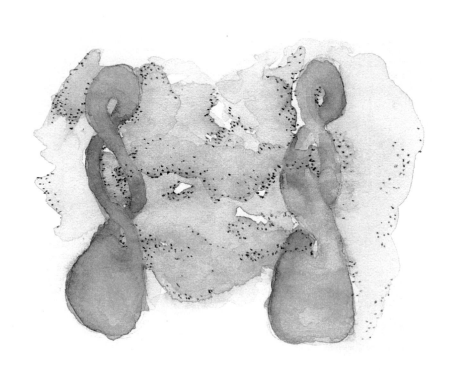

Some family members and others minimize what I am going through and really don't understand.

I honor my journey: I will be patient with those who are grieving in a different way than I am.

We each take a slightly different path to healing. Some have feelings that others don't have or that others find difficult to express. Just as your relationship with your pet was unique, so will be your experience with grief. Honor your healing path as you honor that of others.

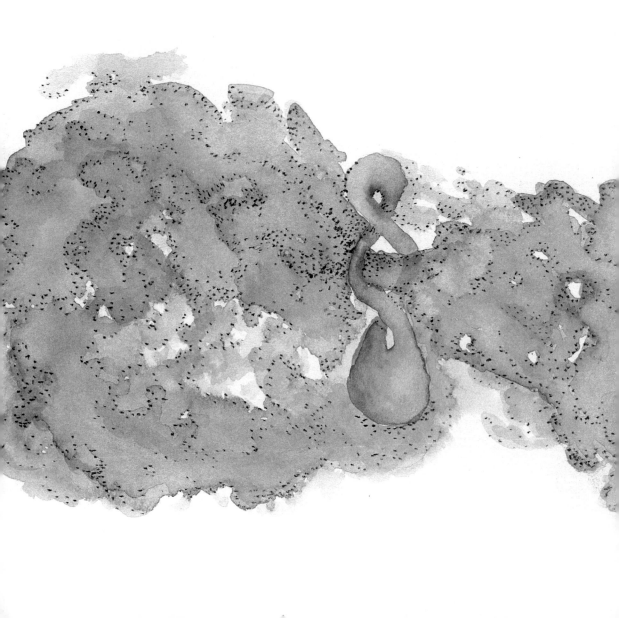

I think I am holding it together, and then I just start to cry. I feel helpless when flooded by emotion.

I honor my journey: I will have self-compassion and be patient with my healing process.

At unpredictable times your feelings may overwhelm you. This is a normal occurrence in the cycle of feelings. Let them ride and be compassionate with yourself. Then change your focus, while still honoring the path.

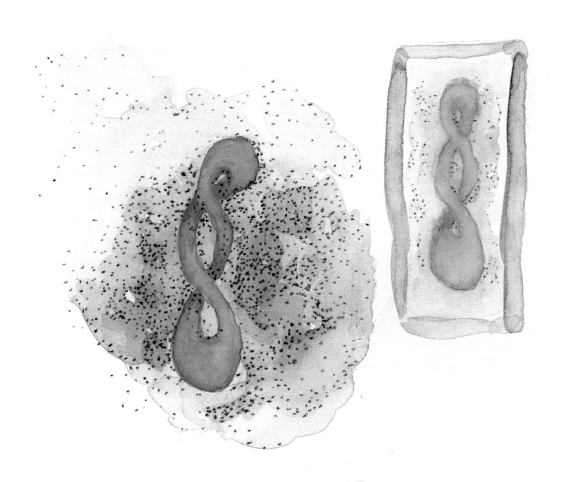

I sometimes feel overwhelmed with the sadness and grief and "forget" who I am.

I honor my journey: I will ask those who know me to remind me of who I am.

Grief is not who you are. It is a path that you are on.

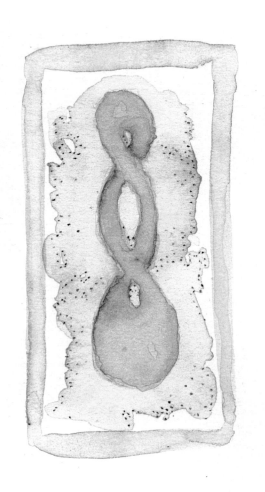

Grief is not who I am. It is a path that I am on.

I honor my journey: I am aware that grief is not who I am but just a path that I am on. I will repeat this page as often as I might need a reminder.

Grief and loss are intense feelings and it is easy to become consumed by them. However, they can also be confused with depression or even bring on a period of clinical depression. If you are identifying grief as who you are and you have difficulty separating yourself from it, then speaking to a professional counselor will help you determine whether you are also having symptoms of depression. See Appendix D if you think you might be having symptoms of clinical depression.

How do I allow myself to grieve as Life around me continues but my life seems to be standing still?

I honor my journey: I allow myself time each day to honor my sadness, grief, and healing. I set aside time to be with my grief and then focus on the other demands of my life.

Our society doesn't offer enough time for us to process our loss, so we must build that time into each day. If you take time to reflect 5 minutes every hour or 30 minutes each morning, you may find it easier to focus on the other demands of your life as they come up. Schedule as much time as you may need. Review the chapter "Memorializing and Taking Care" for ideas.

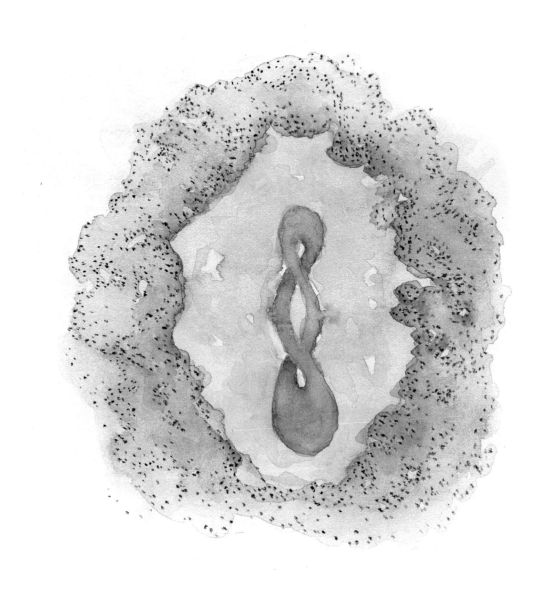

It is hard to feel happy or positive during this time.

I honor my journey by allowing myself to be positive and happy.

Being able to hold the sadness and loss, yet still seeing positive aspects of life and love, allow you to move further down the path of healing. Making yourself focus on these happy or positive aspects of life and the love you shared with your pet prevents you from being stuck in the cloud of grief, while still honoring your grief.

I just want to get on with my life the way it used to be. When will I stop feeling this grief? Does time really heal?

I honor my journey: I do not rush down the path, understanding that time can only heal if I have the courage to walk forward, embracing these feelings, one day at a time.

It is natural to want to hurry feelings of discomfort or sadness. But if your feelings are not fully expressed, they get stuck in the body and psyche and can show up later as illness or emotional trauma. By allowing your emotions to unfold and remaining present where you are, your experience will be transformed and integrated into a new understanding of life.

Breathe.

I honor my journey: I will be still and listen.

Your inner spirit communicates in a still, small voice.

Chapter 2

Memorializing

Nothing is ever lost. That which is excellent
remains forever a part of the universe.

R.W. Emerson

How do I memorialize my pet?

I honor my journey: I memorialize my beloved pet in a way that feels right to me.

Memorializing is a way for you to express the love for your pet and a way of saying goodbye. Memorializing your pet can be accomplished in many ways: creative expression, ceremony, or silent honoring.

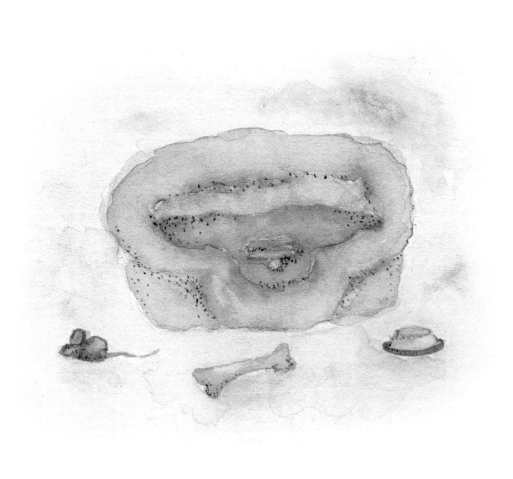

I am saddened by the reminder of my pet's toys, bed, dishes, and other belongings still lying around the house. What do I do with all this stuff?

I honor my journey by putting these items away and replacing these items with pictures and memories of good times, if this feels right for me to do.

Having these items around the house can sometimes elicit a strong emotional response, and in the early stages of loss it is often easier to store them or donate them to a shelter or rescue organization. Alternatively, you may find comfort in leaving things untouched for a short period of time after the loss or designate a place in the house where toys, dishes, collars and pictures can be visited through-out the day.

I still feel the grief. Is memorializing a way to achieve "closure"?

I honor my journey: I know that I can look forward even as I remember the past.

Memorializing your love for the one lost is another step forward on the path of acceptance that your life will be different than how it used to be. It is your cue to begin looking forward, but the healing path is in no way "closed".

A picture says a thousand words...

Although pictures and memories may induce a tear, I honor my journey by looking into those eyes and having the courage to smile.

Photographs of your beloved pet can be carried with you to view, arranged into a collage, or made into a professional portrait or plaque.

I want to personalize the memory.

I honor my journey: I express my love through creative ways of remembrance or representation.

Personalizing can be a powerful way to express your feelings.
• Hold a small ceremony with friends of the deceased.
• Keep the pet tag as a necklace, bracelet or key chain.
• Write a poem or a song about your pet.
• Record memories or write stories about your pet.
• Have others voice record or write stories about your pet.
• Be creative by drawing or painting.
• Plant a tree or a flower.
• Engrave a name plate and fix it to a rock, bench, or tree.
• Make a shadow box of representations of your beloved pet.

None of these ways to memorialize my pet seem right for me.

I honor my journey: I will set aside time every day to be with my thoughts and/or journal my memories to satisfy that longing to connect with my beloved pet.

You may choose a more private way of honoring your beloved pet by lighting a candle daily in silent meditation or walking in silence along a route that your pet enjoyed.

I don't feel that it is necessary for me to labor in a project of expression, but I want to do something in my pet's memory.

I honor my journey: I will know to do as little or as much as I feel is good for me to do.

You may choose to make a financial contribution in your pet's memory.
• Scholarship Funds
• Research Contributions
• Good Samaritan Funds
• Animal Rescue or Welfare Organizations
For a list of organizations and memorials, please refer to the appendix at the end of this book.

Chapter 3

Taking Care

When I loved myself enough I learned to meet
my own needs and not call it selfish.

Kim McMillen

I feel empty. Why am I still consumed by grief?

I honor my journey: I will change my focus from the grief itself to focusing on what I need for support.

Being consumed by a continuous feeling of grief may be an indication that you are not taking care of yourself during a stressful time. Self-nurturing is something most people find difficult. To help identify what may help you, think about how you might help another in your situation. What caring advice might you give? Stop and ask yourself, "What do I need right now?"

It is difficult for me to make it through some days.

I honor my journey: I take care of myself by honoring my spiritual practice of prayer, meditation, or yoga. I call on that which gives me strength.

During times of loss, you can find comfort in knowing that your spiritual Self is always present to support you. All you need to do is quiet your mind and allow the spiritual Breath of peace and strength to see you through, one day at a time.

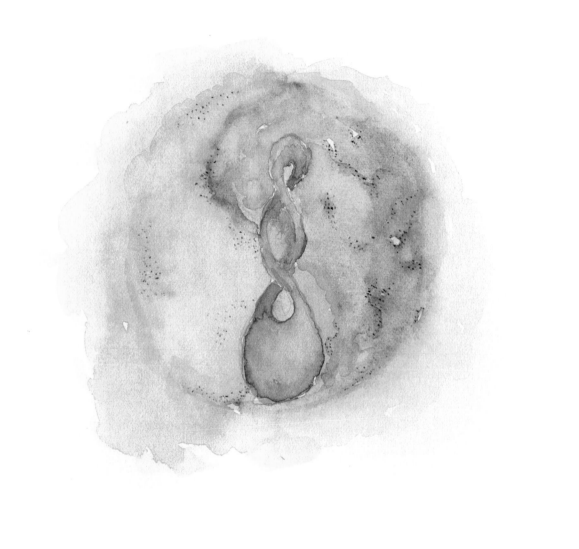

I feel tired, and all I want to do is sleep. It is an effort to exercise as I once did.

I honor my journey: I take care of myself by getting the sleep that I need while continuing my exercise and activities. I will build in more time for me.

Studies show that exercise can reduce stress. Exercise releases endorphins, the body's natural chemicals that elevate your mood. You should take the time you need to sleep, naps included. By combining rest with activity, your mood will be elevated. If you don't usually exercise, start by taking short walks outdoors.

Some days it is more difficult to feel positive.

I will honor where I am on the path while focusing on all that for which I am grateful.

The practice of gratitude can truly elevate your mood. Place your sadness aside and take a moment to focus on all for which you are thankful. Consider writing in a dedicated notebook a daily page of appreciation for all the good that has been and still exists in your life. It is important to not only express the gratefulness but to also fully feel gratitude.

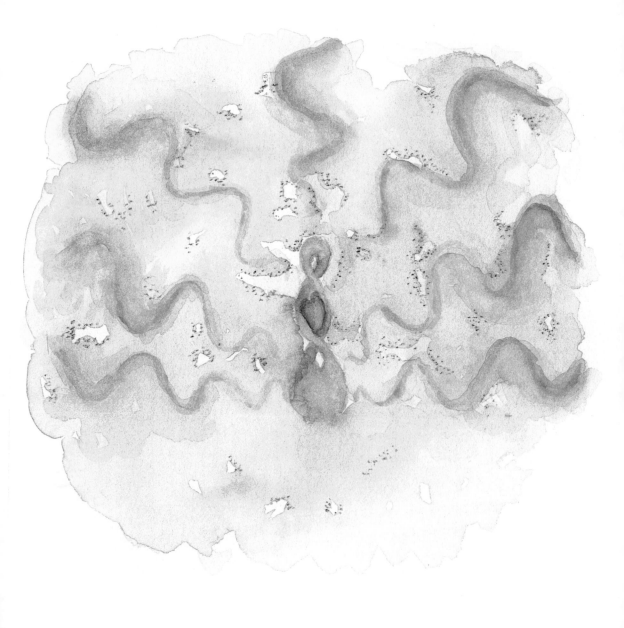

I am tired of feeling sad, but feel guilty to be happy at a time like this.

I honor my journey: I take care of myself by finding something to laugh about.

To laugh is to heal. Laughter can change our feeling state and elevate our physiology from the state of depression caused by grief. You are not dishonoring your loved one by elevating your own mood. Actively seek out a comedic movie or play. Read a comic strip or a book of jokes.

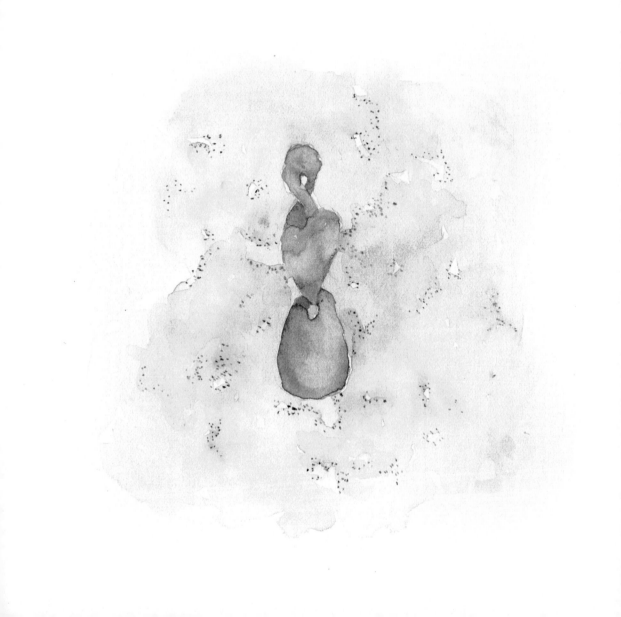

My pet shared a lot with me. How will I ever feel the same about the activities we shared? I don't feel like doing anything.

I honor my journey: I will do something special for myself at least once per week.

It is easy to find yourself so consumed by your grief that you stop doing the things that you previously enjoyed in your life. During times of loss, pay special attention to plan self-nurturing activities. Now is the time to focus on other things besides the path. You are still honoring your sorrow while you also acknowledge the other aspects of you that must not be forgotten.

- Enjoy a massage.
- Reward yourself with an affordable gift.
- Treat yourself to a nutritious, tasty meal at your favorite restaurant.
- Take a spa day and relax by the pool.
- Attend a cultural event.
- Sit by the fire with a good book and homemade cookies.
- Go to the playground with a child.
- Plan a hike or a long walk with a friend.

I miss the connection I had with my pet, but I am not ready to get another pet yet.

I honor my journey: I will keep connected with the animal kingdom.

You may want to go to a zoo, visit an animal reserve, or make a point to visit a friend with pets. You might take this one step further and actually donate time to help at a rescue organization or an animal shelter. It is important to not push yourself into getting another animal too soon, yet it is just as important to avail yourself to receive joy from the animal kingdom.

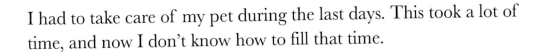

I had to take care of my pet during the last days. This took a lot of time, and now I don't know how to fill that time.

I honor my journey: I will add something to my life to fill the time that used to be occupied by my pet.

Nursing a pet's chronic illness can occupy a lot of time and focus. Finding other activities can help you reinvest in your life until you are ready to bring another life into your focus. Consider taking that long-awaited vacation to re-energize yourself.

I sometimes feel depleted of energy. Why am I so worn down?

I honor my journey: I will seek out activities that actively recharge me.

Paying attention to the simple joys in life can open your awareness from the often narrowed scope of loss. Watch a sunrise or sunset, visit a place that you love (the mountains, the beach, a botanical garden or a park), or maybe just stop and smell the roses.

I seem to do OK when I am at work or when I keep myself busy, but when I am alone, I think too much and tend to get sad.

I honor my journey: I will reach for thoughts and feelings that make me feel better, knowing I am still honoring my journey.

Shifting your thoughts and feelings to the happy times with your pet will elevate your mood and allow you to look forward, thereby moving you forward on the path of healing.

- Reminisce with a friend or family member about a funny event you had with your pet.
- Try to re-create the uplifting feeling you had when you were playing with your pet.
- Remember the tail wagging or the loud purring of contentment.
- Smile and feel the peace and joy of those moments spent cuddling your pet.

It is such an effort to engage life again.

I honor my journey: I will engage life by beginning to look forward and dream.

Knowing that your feelings on this path are transient and believing in a brighter tomorrow opens the door to transformation. Engage life by stargazing, window shopping, and daydreaming.

I loved my pet so much! I truly miss that connection.

I honor my journey by knowing and feeling the love that my pet mirrored back to me.

Your pet gave you unconditional love, mirroring the love you gave to him or her. This reflection of love is always accessible since the source of that love lies within you. Allow yourself to bask in the beauty of this love.

Chapter 4

Evaluation

Self-knowledge leads to transformation.
Rebuilding is a gift!

KaLee R. Pasek, DVM

I honor my journey: I will evaluate the feelings and the meanings of the loss that I am experiencing.

I honor my journey by taking time to use this section as a tool for self discovery. By journaling the exercises in this section, I will move my experience through the Forest of Sorrow into the Field of Transformation.

Each loss is different. Each pet brings to you a different relationship and therefore a qualitatively different experience. By examining what elements existed in your relationship, you can move down the path with more growth and understanding about yourself, your relationship with your pet, and your relationship with your grief.

I honor my journey: I will recall a list of unique qualities about my beloved pet.

Loyal

Full of Life

Stubborn

Sweet

Happy

Strong Willed

Playful

Goofy

Gentle

Affectionate

Comforting

Mischievous

Shy

Anxious

Curious

Peaceful

Brave

Vocal

Your pet lived in the Now, authentically expressing these qualities of Being. Your pet's qualities might have mirrored some of your own qualities or they may be qualities which you found difficulty expressing. By recalling and remembering them, you can explore how being exposed to these qualities touched your life and find ways to bring more of them into your life now.

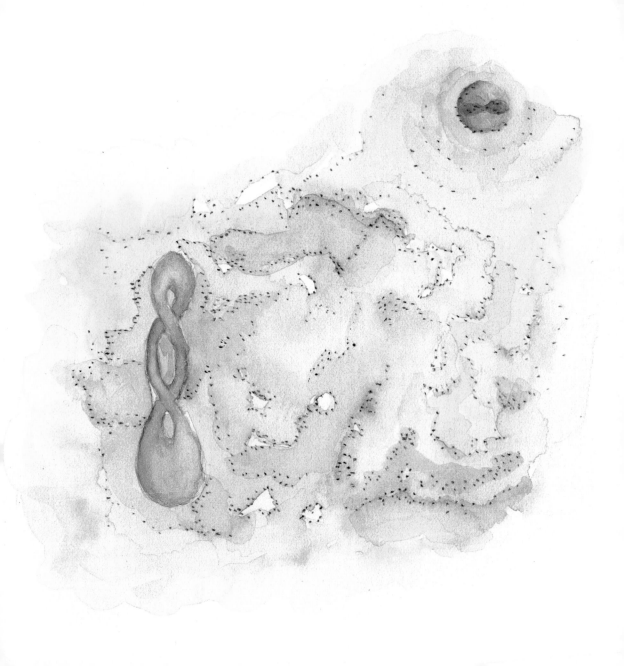

I honor my journey: I will list the feelings and experiences my beloved pet brought to my life.

Companionship

Belongingness

Social Interactions

Exercise

Safety

The Experience of Taking Care of Another as One Might a Child

Youthfulness

Giving and Receiving Love

Comfort

Total Acceptance

Responsibility

Support

Feelings of Being Connected to a Past Loved One

Joy and Happiness

Working Partner

The Feeling of Being Needed

Pleasure

By giving unconditional love, your pet might have been more than just a companion. It is important to recognize the other wonderful roles he or she played in your life. By understanding this, you realize the additional impact of loss on your life. This loss must also be honored. But also realize that although your pet brought these experiences into your life in such a beautiful and selfless way, new ways of fulfilling these elements will need to be explored.

I honor my journey: I will recognize the part of my life that my pet walked with me.

Loss of a Friend

Childhood and Adolescent Years

Marriage and Divorce

Emotional Event

First Job

First Love

Illness and Recovery

College

Moving Across Country

Job Change

Relationship Breakup

Starting a New Business

Difficult Financial Times

Death of a Parent

Changing Residence

The timing of your pet's loss can coincide with the loss of a marriage, the loss of a job, the loss of your youth, or some other important event in your life. Your pet lived a chapter of your life and frequently their death represents an end to this chapter. This can add to the impact of the grief you are experiencing. Acknowledging this connection will help you assimilate some of the intensity of the feelings.

I honor my journey: I will recognize the significance of this loss as it may stimulate the feelings of other losses in my life.

Loss of a parent

Loss of a Previous Pet

Loss of a Friend   *Loss of a Spouse*   *Loss of a Job*

Loss of your Health

Loss of a Child

Loss of a Marriage

Loss of a Partner

Loss of a Promotion

Loss of a Living Condition or Lifestyle

Commonly, one loss can trigger the feelings of other losses that have occurred in your life. It is important to recognize that your current grief might be complicated by unresolved grief about a person in your life or circumstances surrounding the death of another pet. Exploring this possibility will loosen those losses that might be tangled in the current emotions, moving you farther down the path to healing.

I honor my journey: I will write a letter to my pet expressing anything that I am sorry about, that I must forgive, or that which I wish to express.

I am sorry things got so complicated.   *I wish my finances allowed me to do more.*

I loved you and never wished to see you suffer.

I am so sorry for getting so angry.

I forgive you for eating my shoes.   *I am sorry that I yelled at you.*

I understand you couldn't help it when you messed in the house.

I miss you so much.   *I am sorry I ignored you when you wanted to be petted.*

I wish I had more time to spend with you.

Sorry I was too busy to play every night.

I wish I could have been there to say good bye.

I am sorry I pushed you away when you wanted to cuddle.

I wish I could hug you now.   *I will never forget you.*

The act of releasing thoughts and feelings that are tied up inside of you can be a cleansing exercise. It is important to release and not dwell, knowing that everything that you expressed is accepted by you and your pet. Share your letter with a trusted friend or loved one who also knew your pet.

I honor my journey: I will use this evaluation section as a tool for my healing. I will journal my progress.

I am still sad, but I am also happy that I had such a close relationship with my pet.

I will miss our time together.   *I am happy we shared so much together.*

I never knew that I could love an animal this much.

Pets give unconditional love.

I see the gifts my pet left behind and have identified the qualities I desire more of in my life.

Although this process has been difficult to bear, I am more confident that I will see it through.

Journaling your progress and "talking" to yourself about how you feel helps you express where you are on the path. By reviewing your journal, you can see the healing progress you have made and the lessons you have gained from this experience.

Chapter 5

Healing

One word frees us from all the weight and pain of life:
That word is LOVE.

Sophocles

I honor my journey:

I am being called forward out of my grief and can see
the sunlight on the horizon.

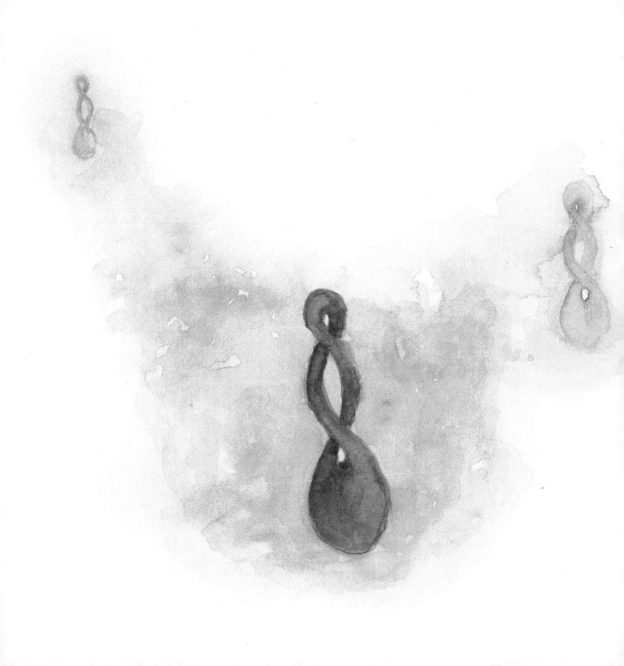

I honor my journey:

I am becoming more aware of today and tomorrow.
Yesterday is distancing itself.

I honor my journey:

I have the courage and willingness to take action, move forward, and set aside the preoccupation of grief.

I honor my journey:

I have learned that during my darkest hour, I can transform darkness into glimmers of light.

I honor my journey:

I know my life is different now, and I embrace it.

I honor my journey:

I can find deep within me the strength to see things through.

I honor my journey:

I trust the newness, the newness of me.

I honor my journey:

I have demonstrated how deeply I am able to love.

I honor my journey:

I have become more aware of my relationship with my pet as Love, lessening the pain of my relationship with grief and feelings of despair.

I honor my journey:

I realize now all of the wonderful gifts that little
soul brought to my life.

I honor my journey:

I can experience the gift of pure positive energy and Being, which is one of the many gifts I received by sharing this bond with my pet.

I honor my journey:

I appreciate the unconditional love my pet gave
to me on a daily basis.

I honor my journey:

I know that my love for my pet extends beyond the boundaries of space and time.

I honor my journey:

I understand that loss is an extension of the love I have for my pet.

I honor my journey:

I realize that my pet is an extension of the love that I have for myself.

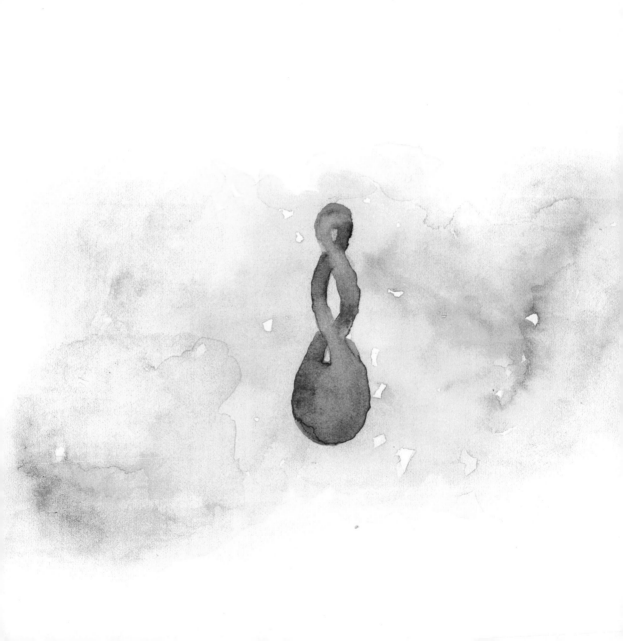

I honor my journey:

I see that the relationship I had with my pet is an extension of the relationship I have with myself.

I honor my journey:

I have a greater appreciation for the preciousness
of life and relationships.

I honor my journey

I realize that grief can grow into periods of personal transformation.

I honor my journey:

Instead of clinging, I now honor the past and allow
new experiences into my life.

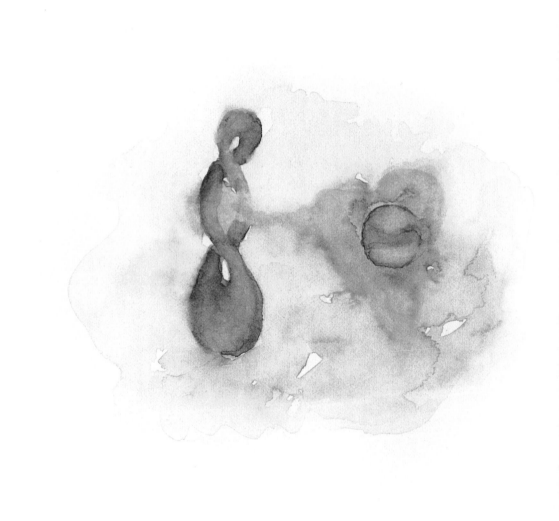

I honor my journey:

I know I can share my love with another.

I honor my journey:

I give gratitude and thanks for the love I have for my pet.

Place your
pet's photo
here

THANK YOU, _____,
(your pet's name)

FOR SHARING YOUR LIFE WITH ME!

Appendices

Appendix A: Reading List
Loss, Death, and the Grief Process

Anderson, Allen and Linda -
Saying Goodbye to Your Angel Animals; Finding Comfort After Losing Your Pet
New World Library, 2005.

Anderson, M. - *Coping with Sorrow on the Loss of Your Pet*
Second Edition, Peregrine Press 1996.

Barton Ross, Cheri & Baron-Sorensen, Jane - *Pet Loss and Human Emotion*
Taylor & Francis Group, 1998.

Davis, C., (Illustrator) - *For Every Dog an Angel: The Forever Dog*
Lighthearted Press,1997.

Grollman, E. - *Talking About Death: A Dialogue Between Parents and Children*
Putnam/Beacon Press, 1990.

Harris, Julia A. - *Pet Loss: A Spiritual Guide*
Lantern Books, 2002.

Holt, Peggy R. - *All My Children Wear Fur Coats*
Infinity Publishing, 2002.

Hunt, Laurel E. -
Angel Pawprints: Reflections On Loving and Losing a Canine Companion
Hyperion, 2000.

James, John & Friedman, Russell - *The Grief Recovery Handbook*
Harper Collins, 1998.

Kowalski, G. -
Goodbye Friend: Healing Wisdom for Anyone Who Has Ever Lost a Pet
Stillpoint Publishing, 1997.

Kumar, Sameet M. -
Grieving Mindfully: A Compassionate and Spiritual Guide to Coping With Loss
New Harbinger Publications, Inc., 2005.

Morehead, D. -
A Special Place For Charlie: A Child's Companion Through Pet Loss
Partners in Publishing, LLC, 1996.

Osmont, K. - *More Than Surviving: Caring For Yourself While You Grieve*
Centering Corporation, 1990.

Rylant, Cynthia - *Cat Heaven (and Dog Heaven)*
Scholastic Books, 1997.

Schweibert, Pat & Deklyen, Chuck - *Tear Soup-A Recipe For Healing After Loss*
Perinatal Loss Publications, 2001.

Shelton, Mary M. -
Guidance From the Darkness-How to Thrive Through Difficult Times
Jeremy P. Tarcher / Putnam a member of Penguin Putnam Inc., 2004.

Sife, Wallace -
The Loss of a Pet: A Guide to Coping with the Grieving Process When a Pet Dies
Howell Book House, 2005.

Steinbach, D. -
Loving, Caring, Letting Go Without Guilt: A Compassionate but Straightforward Look at Pet Euthanasia
Willow Ben Publishing, 1997.

Tousley, M. - *Children and Pet Loss: A Guide for Helping*
Pals Publishing, 1996.

Tousley, M., & Heuerman, K. -
The Final Farewell: Preparing for and Mourning the Loss of Your Pet
Pals Publishing, 1997.

Viorst, Judith - *The Tenth Good Thing About Barney*
Atheneum, 1975.

Appendix B: Pet Loss Support Services

Animal Bereavement Support Group	www.agapelive.com/index.php?page=217
Animal Kinship Spiritual and Emotional Support	1-310-348-1206 x 1281
Animal Love & Loss Network	www.alln.org
Association of Pet Loss and Bereavement	www.aplb.org
ASPCA	1-212-876-7700
AVMA-American Veterinary Medical Association	1-888-478-7574 www.avma.org/care4pets/lossandi.htm
Certified Grief Recovery Specialist –Dr. Kathleen Ayl	1-805-856-8466
Colorado State University	1-970-297-1242
Companion Animal Association of Arizona	1-602-995-5885
Cornell University	1-607-253-3932 www.vewt.cornell.edu/public/petloss
IAMS Company Pet Loss	1-888-332-7738
Iowa State Pet Loss Group	1-888-478-7574
Michigan State University	1-517-432-2696

Pet Bereavement Resource	www.catanddoghelp.com/animals/bereavment.php
Pet Bereavement Support	1-561-272-6322
Pet Loss Grief Support and Candle Ceremony	www.petloss.com
Pet Loss Support	www.pet-loss.com
Rainbow Bridge Tribute Page	www.bestfriends.org
Tufts University	1-508-839-7966 6pm-9pm 1-508-839-5302 mainline
UC DAVIS	1-800-565-1526 1-530-752-3602 1-530-752-7295 anytime
University of Florida	1-904-338-2031
University of Illinois	www.vetmed.illinois.edu/CARE

Appendix C: Pet Memorials/Tributes

ASPCA Memorial Page-Make a Memory

www.aspca.org

AVMA/Pet Memories

1-800-248-2862 x6689
www.avmf.org/avmf

Heifer Int'l Ending Hunger

1-800-422-0474
www.heifer.org

Plant a Tree in Loving Memory

1-877-245-7378
www.celebrationforest.com

Tree Givers/Pet Memorials

1-800-862-8733
www.treegivers.com

Comfort Company Remembrance Ornaments/Keepsakes   www.thecomfortcompany.net

Delta Society

1-425-226-7357
www.deltasociety.org/PetLossRemember.htm

In Memory of Pets-Beyond Life's Gateway

www.in-memory-of-pets.com

Humane Society of the USA

1-202-452-1100
www.hsus.org/pets/

Marty's Column

www.ourpals.com

Morris Foundation

1-800-243-2345

Pet Loss Memorials   www.foreverpets.com

Pet Urns   www.theurnist.com

UC Davis University of California Memorial Program   1-916-752-7024

Unique Animal Gourds   info@foothillpethospital.com
  Fine Oils of Exotic Birds & Flowers
  Feather Masks
  Hand Painted Glass Objects

Fur, Feathers, & Fins Studio   1-866-393-7111
  Dawn Secord, Artist   www.DawnSecord.com

Appendix D

Clinical depression can be a serious condition. Feeling these expressions on occasion can be normal and can be a part of the loss process, especially during early grief. Feeling them consistently over a steady period of time can indicate clinical depression. Please talk to a health professional if you feel the majority of these statements are consistent with your feelings.

I feel like my life is over.

I don't think I can make it another day.

The pain is so intense that I can't stop crying.

I don't see that I have anything else to live for.

I am having difficulty feeling the love and support others are offering.

I don't want to be around anyone. I feel like isolating myself from everyone.

I am not hungry and I have to make myself eat. Or. I can't stop eating.

I am having insomnia. Or. I can't wake up…all I want to do is sleep.

I feel so guilty that I can hardly face myself.

I feel worthless and don't feel like I contribute much at all.

I can't think straight or concentrate and routine tasks are an effort.

Nothing seems to help how I am feeling.

I can't plan to do anything. I can hardly plan the rest of today.

I don't see how things could possibly get better.

It would be easier if I just give up.

This is one thing you can take control of. Make the call!

23070813R00094

Made in the USA
San Bernardino, CA
03 August 2015